CLASSIC PIANO REPERTOIRE
JOHN THOMPSON

12 MASTERFUL PIANO SOLOS

ISBN 978-1-4768-8958-0

WILLIS MUSIC

EXCLUSIVELY DISTRIBUTED BY

HAL•LEONARD®
CORPORATION
7777 W. BLUEMOUND RD. P.O. BOX 13819 MILWAUKEE, WI 53213

Visit Hal Leonard Online at
www.halleonard.com

"I think I first knew I was going to be interested in music when I learned my first piece in the **JOHN THOMPSON** book. Everybody who's ever taken piano lessons has to take a John Thompson course."

"I grew up learning **JOHN THOMPSON's** pieces. I loved them then, and I love them still – I could not have asked for a better beginning! Basic concepts were soundly introduced, but in the most charming way so that I was always eager for more. The wonderful thing about Thompson's pieces is that they teach the crucial pianistic skills, so progress is assured."

JOHN THOMPSON (1889-1963) was born in Williamstown, Pennsylvania, the eldest of four children of James and Emma Thompson. He began music study at the age of five, and his parents encouraged his prodigious talent by sending him to study piano with Maurits Leefson at the Leefson-Hille Conservatory in Philadelphia, graduating in 1909. At the same time, he studied composition with Dr. Hugh Clark at the University of Pennsylvania. In his early twenties Thompson toured the United States and Europe as a concert pianist, receiving respectable reviews and performing with several European orchestras. He was in London when the start of World War I abruptly ended his concert career. After his return to the United States, he began a distinguished career as a pedagogue, heading music conservatories in Indianapolis, Philadelphia, as well as the Kansas City Conservatory of Music (now University of Missouri at Kansas City). It was during these tenures that he developed his distinctive ideas about teaching young children and adults and began his prolific composing and publishing career.

His best-selling method books *Teaching Little Fingers to Play* and *Modern Course for the Piano* were first published by the Willis Music Company in the mid-1930s and soon grew to include the *Easiest Piano Course* and other notable educational publications. These publications have had a profound influence on millions of musicians today, and continue to have an impact on the teaching of piano in America and throughout the world.

FROM THE PUBLISHERS

The *Classic Piano Repertoire* series includes popular as well as lesser-known pieces from a select group of composers out of the Willis piano archives (established in 1899). This volume features 12 original piano solos by John Thompson ranging from early intermediate to early advanced. Each piece has been newly engraved and edited with the aim to preserve Thompson's primary intent and musical purpose.

Of special interest is the fact that several Thompson pieces were initially published under pseudonyms. For the purpose of this book, every piece is properly credited to Thompson.

CONTENTS

John Thompson, age 28.

Valse Chromatique

John Thompson

2nd Time to Coda

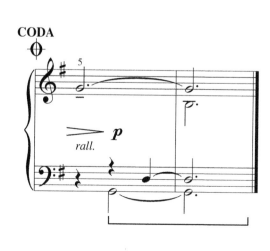

Tango Carioca

John Thompson

Nocturne

John Thompson

Andantino, molto espressivo

The Faun

John Thompson

Playfully

2nd Time to Coda

The Juggler
(Staccato Caprice)

John Thompson

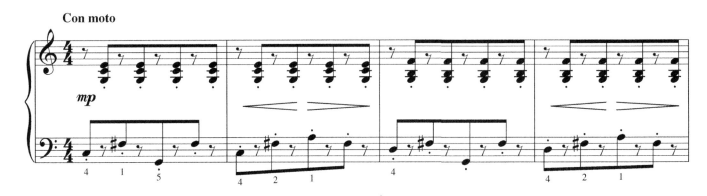

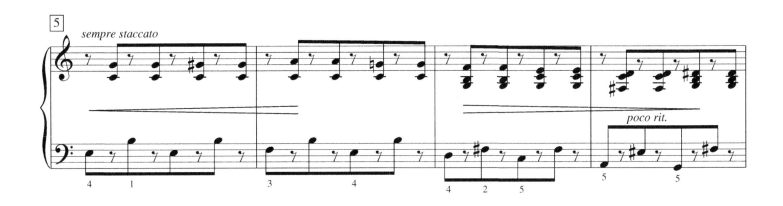

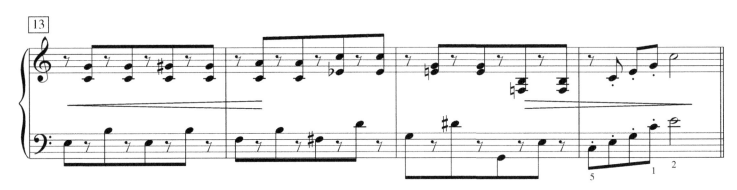

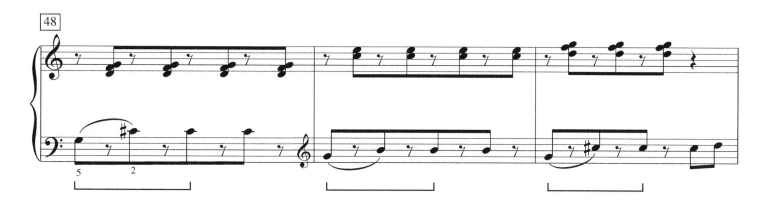

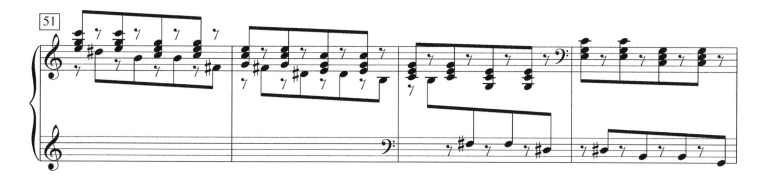

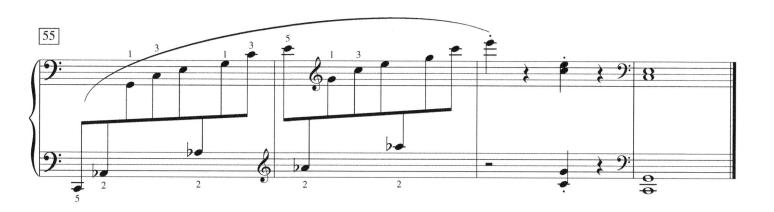

To my good friend Carl W. Yager

Lagoon

John Thompson

Andantino con moto

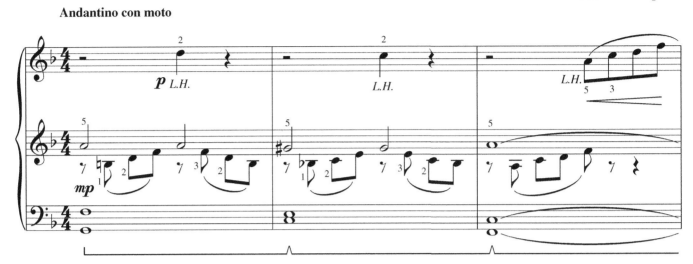

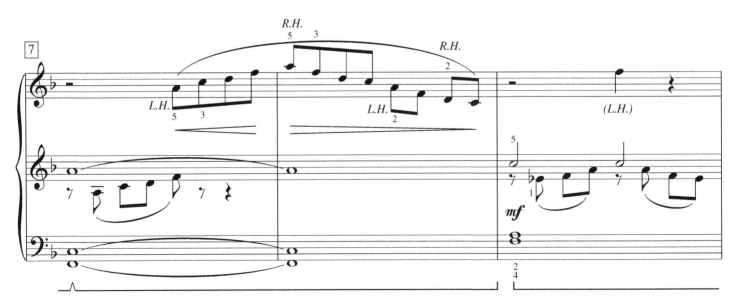

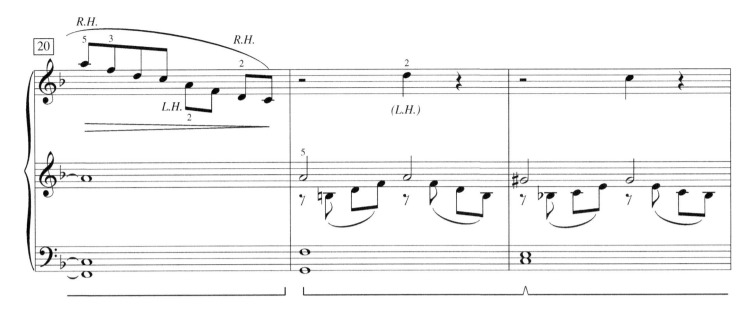

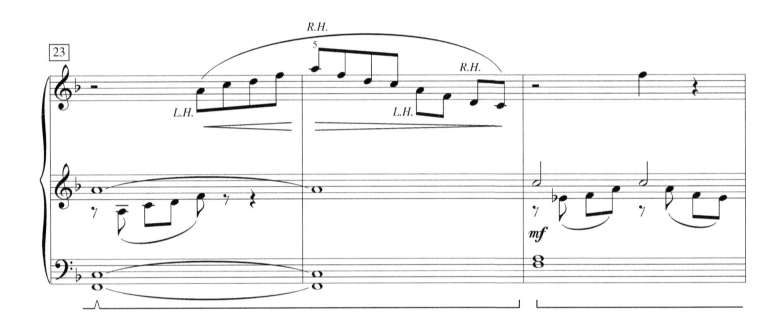

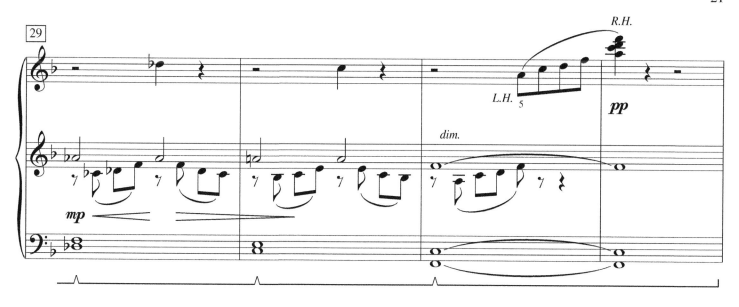

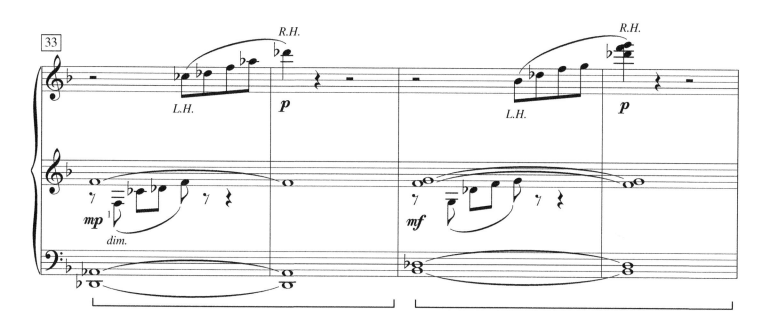

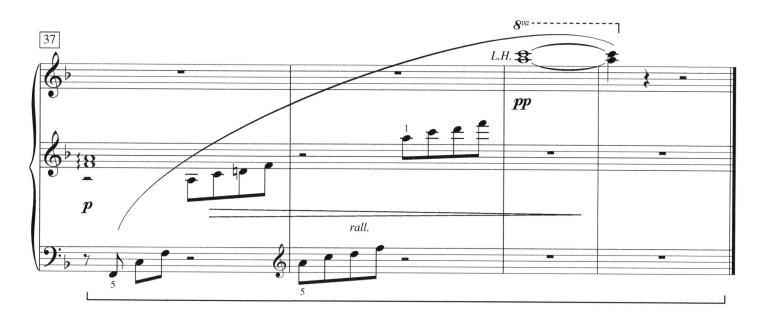

Lofty Peaks

John Thompson

Scherzando in G Major

John Thompson

* Also published as "The Fairies' Frolic."

* Sharp added.

The Coquette

John Thompson

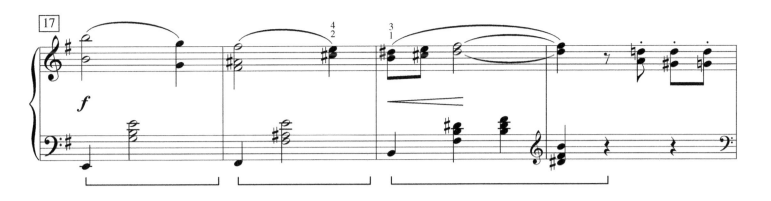

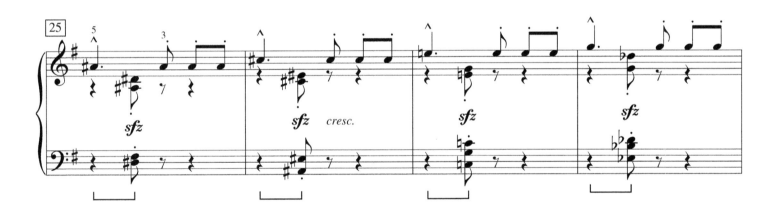

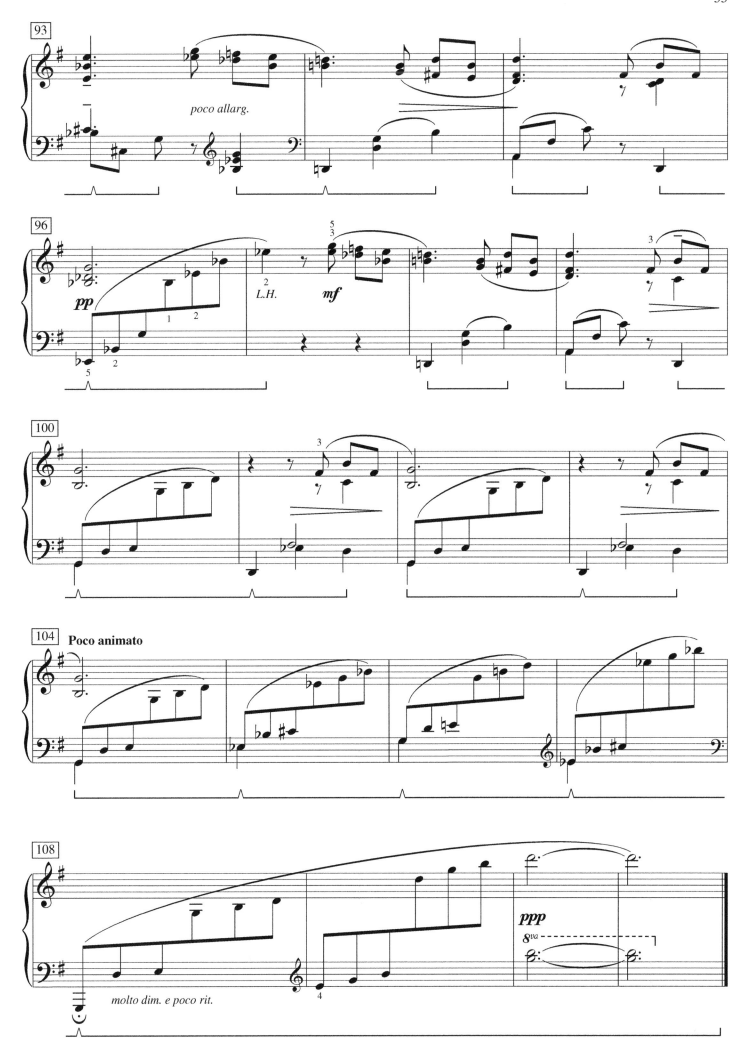

Andantino
from CONCERTO IN D MINOR

John Thompson

Arranged for Piano Solo by John Thompson

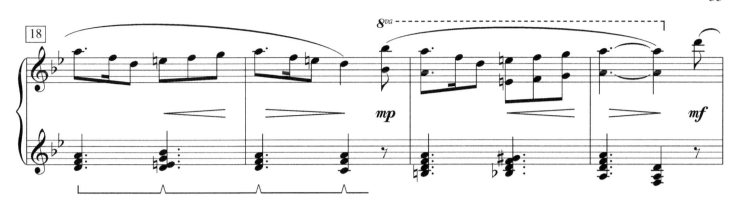

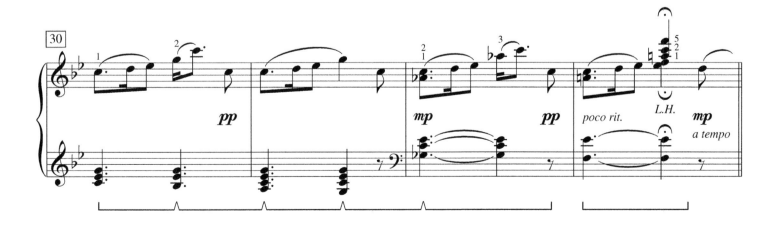

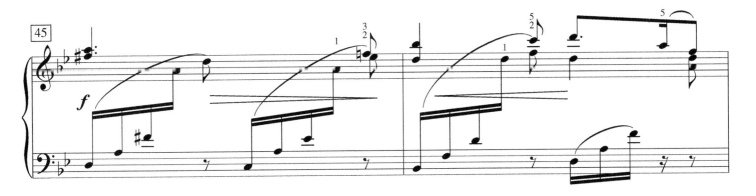

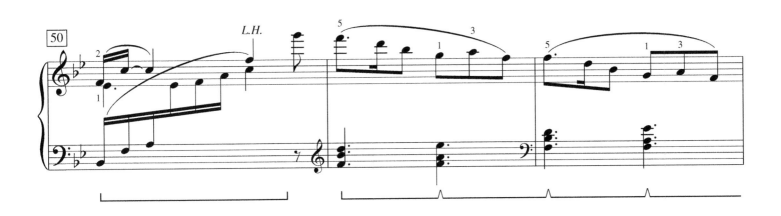

Valse Burlesque

John Thompson

Rhapsodie Hongroise

John Thompson

CLASSIC PIANO REPERTOIRE

The *Classic Piano Repertoire* series includes popular as well as lesser-known pieces from a select group of composers out of the Willis piano archives. Every piece has been newly engraved and edited with the aim to preserve each composer's original intent and musical purpose.

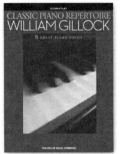

WILLIAM GILLOCK – ELEMENTARY

8 Great Piano Solos

Dance in Ancient Style • Little Flower Girl of Paris • On a Paris Boulevard • Rocking Chair Blues • Sliding in the Snow • Spooky Footsteps • A Stately Sarabande • Stormy Weather.

00416957 ....$8.99

EDNA MAE BURNAM – ELEMENTARY

8 Great Piano Solos

The Clock That Stopped • The Friendly Spider • A Haunted House • New Shoes • The Ride of Paul Revere • The Singing Cello • The Singing Mermaid • Two Birds in a Tree.

00110228 ....$8.99

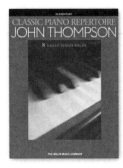

JOHN THOMPSON – ELEMENTARY

9 Great Piano Solos

Captain Kidd • Drowsy Moon • Dutch Dance • Forest Dawn • Humoresque • Southern Shuffle • Tiptoe • Toy Ships • Up in the Air.

00111968 ....$8.99

LYNN FREEMAN OLSON – EARLY TO LATER ELEMENTARY

14 Great Piano Solos

Caravan • Carillon • Come Out! Come Out! (Wherever You Are) • Halloween Dance • Johnny, Get Your Hair Cut! • Jumping the Hurdles • Monkey on a Stick • Peter the Pumpkin Eater • Pony Running Free • Silent Shadows • The Sunshine Song • Tall Pagoda • Tubas and Trumpets • Winter's Chocolatier.

00294722 ....$9.99

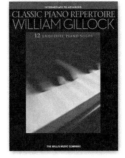

WILLIAM GILLOCK – INTERMEDIATE TO ADVANCED

12 Exquisite Piano Solos

Classic Carnival • Etude in A Major (The Coral Sea) • Etude in E Minor • Etude in G Major (Toboggan Ride) • Festive Piece • A Memory of Vienna • Nocturne • Polynesian Nocturne • Sonatina in Classic Style • Sonatine • Sunset • Valse Etude.

00416912 .... $12.99

EDNA MAE BURNAM – INTERMEDIATE TO ADVANCED

13 Memorable Piano Solos

Butterfly Time • Echoes of Gypsies • Hawaiian Leis • Jubilee! • Longing for Scotland • Lovely Senorita • The Mighty Amazon River • Rumbling Rumba • The Singing Fountain • Song of the Prairie • Storm in the Night • Tempo Tarantelle • The White Cliffs of Dover.

00110229 .... $12.99

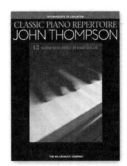

JOHN THOMPSON – INTERMEDIATE TO ADVANCED

12 Masterful Piano Solos

Andantino (from Concerto in D Minor) • The Coquette • The Faun • The Juggler • Lagoon • Lofty Peaks • Nocturne • Rhapsody Hongroise • Scherzando in G Major • Tango Carioca • Valse Burlesque • Valse Chromatique.

00111969 .... $12.99

LYNN FREEMAN OLSON – EARLY TO MID-INTERMEDIATE

13 Distinctive Piano Solos

Band Wagon • Brazilian Holiday • Cloud Paintings • Fanfare • The Flying Ship • Heroic Event • In 1492 • Italian Street Singer • Mexican Serenade • Pageant Dance • Rather Blue • Theme and Variations • Whirlwind.

00294720 ....$9.99